# GOLFERS HANDBOOK
## Save your golf game- and your LIFE!

**Photography:** Linda Dögg Guðmundsdóttir
**Video Intro:** Tommy Pedersen
**Videography & Editing:** Kristoffer Rishøj & Adam Stevenson
**Video- & Photo Locations:** Sindal Golfklub, Løkken Golfklub, Hjørring Golfklub, Hjørring Bibliotek
**Layout:** Vestergaards Bogtrykkeri
**Model & Toe Toucher p. 14-15:** Jim Magill
**Model, Roller, Deep-squatter, & Future golfstar p. 10-11:** Isabella Guðmundsdóttir
**Author:** Adam Stevenson - with advice and material on nutrition and energy from expert Pernille H. Steenberg

# This is a SMART book!

In this book there are video demonstrations that are accessible via QR codes for use with your smartphones or tablets . Simply download a QR scanner (for example Microsoft Tag app.), scan the code and watch the video.
If your version of this book is in eBook format, simply click on the QR code image with your touch screen or click on it with your mouse.

You can start by touch/scan the QR code below!

*This book is meant to be a tool to help accelerate golfers understanding of how they can perform at a higher level by improving their golf game and their way of life. The people associated with this book are in no way liable for injuries to people reading this book.*

# FOREWORD

Adam Stevenson has always been a seeker of knowledge. He hungers for comprehension of complex concepts in golf performance.
His hunger is not for his own satiation but instead his mission is to feed others with his new found knowledge.

Adam has an amazing ability to take these complex concepts and break them down into easily digestible bites for the beginner, intermediate and elite golfer. This book is exactly that! Everything a golfer needs to take their golf game to the next level.
Adam does an fantastic job of connecting the golf swing to the body and the body to the golf swing.

I love this book and I am honoured to have Adam as a colleague and a friend.

*Jason Glass BHK CSCS TPI Advisory Board*

http://www.jasonglassperformancelab.com

# Table of contents

| | | |
|---|---|---|
| **Chapter 1:** | Departure on TIME! (checking in) | 4 |
| **Chapter 2:** | Move your body (the nitty-gritty of it all) | 9 |
| **Chapter 3:** | Know YOUR body (the meat and potatoes) | 25 |
| **Chapter 4:** | Unlocking YOUR golf swings potential | 53 |
| **Chapter 5:** | GREAT body...GREAT golf swing (Kapow'r) | 63 |
| **Chapter 6:** | Get your motor started | 73 |
| **Chapter 7:** | Nutrition & Energy w/ Pernille H. Steenberg | 80 |
| **Chapter 8:** | The mental game (getting out of your own way) | 101 |
| **Chapter 9:** | Arrival on TIME (checking out) | 104 |

"If you think you can, you can.
If you think you can't, you're right"
- Henry Ford, Ford Motor Company

# Chapter 1:
# Departure on time! *(Checking in)*

Golf is an enjoyable sport that has all the ingredients required in achieving a recipe for happiness. While playing a round of golf you are exercising out in nature while getting the fresh air you need. You are playing on green grass and with a little luck there is plenty of sunshine. Golf can be a social and competitive sport and if played well golf can give you great self-satisfaction. All these elements combined together help produce a natural chemical in your brain called endorphin, which can help you stay positive and energetic. What could be better, right? However, in the game of golf we do keep track of how many shots we have used, which often leads to expectations. We start to evaluate our round on how well we hit the ball and how many strokes we have used to get the ball in the hole. Frustrations start to build up, taking a toll on our deposit of endorphins, depleting it, and as a result, making it difficult to maintain a positive attitude throughout our round. In order to live up to your expectations and perform at your best, you will need to maintain your endorphin deposits and a positive attitude. How? Here's how, realizing that no matter how old you are, or which level of experience you play golf at, YOU are an athlete.

An athlete is a person that plays a sport that requires a specific movement pattern of the body that is controlled by your brain, which results in how well the sport is played.

Think of your body as the "motor" of your golf swing, and your brain as the control panel controlling what your body does.

In this book I will teach you what is required for you to fine tune your motor, and if you put in a little elbow grease, you will get overhauled and perhaps even have a turbo installed in your motor.

Pernille will help make sure that your control panel receives the correct fuel to keep your motor firing on all cylinders for 18 holes, which will also help you maintain a positive and energetic attitude throughout the day.

With our experience we know that the correct body movement and nutrition are two of the most important factors when improving an avid golfer. These are two hugely important ingredients the pros have known and taken advantage of for years. Still somehow this knowledge has tragically eluded everyday golfers until NOW!

Now please sit back and close your eyes and ask yourself the following question:

**Do I want to play more consistant golf, have improved shot control, more length, prevent injury, and at the same time, increased concentration and confidence on and off the course?**

If your answer is yes, then congratulations, you are being honest with yourself! I have never met a golfer that did not want to improve, though I have met a golfer that did not believe they could…but we will get back to that later!

If you want to improve you will need to stop wasting your time with poor swing movements that leave you hitting poor shots, and can potentially cause injury but instead learn about who YOU are and how YOU can improve your golf game.

This book has one simple philosophy, as an athlete, you will first need to earn the right to improve. You will need to learn what your body can or cannot do, learn how to improve any dysfunctions, and eliminate any limitations. Only then can you unleash your true golf potential and effectively move your body correctly to increase shot distance, consistency and prevent risk of injury. This philosophy will also benefit your quality of life on a daily basis.

If all this sounds too good to be true, or maybe you think it is too ambitious a goal for you….WHY? It is never too late to get started!

Your body and your mind have something in common, if you do not use them, you will lose them!

Dare to improve, and to be the best you can be! Because when it comes to living you only have three choices: **Give up, give in, or give it all you've got!!!!!**

# Coach Adam

Adam Stevenson was born in Canada, but moved to Denmark in the late 90's. Today he is one of Denmarks most dedicated golf coaches with a vast knowledge and understanding of how the body works in the golf swing to produce maximum results. He is able to breakdown the golf swings DNA through understanding both physically and technically how it works. At the same time he is able to adapt his knowledge and expertise to the individual need of each golfer. Adam is a PGA Professional[2] and is a TPI certified expert[3] on both the fitness and medical sides of the TPI educational program. Adam actively participates and believes in on-going education and in his words is a "student for life".

Adams mission is quite simply to help golfers at all levels and ages improve and learn a healthier and more efficient golf swing and as a bonus have a better quality of life. For Adam golf is a passion, and it is that passion he wants to share with you.

http://www.adamstevensongolf.com

2. Professional Golfers Association (www.PGA.dk)
3. Titleist Performance Institute (www.myTPI.com)

# Chapter 2:
# MOVE YOUR BODY! *(The nitty-gritty)*

Often when receiving instruction either through a lesson, reading golf instruction in a book or magazine or seeing a video from an expert, you are told to "***just*** do this" or "***just*** do that". It may not be that these tips are incorrect, but they could be incorrect for you! You try to implement these changes but they do not seem to improve your game. As time goes by you unknowingly fall back to the same swing you are used to, which means you have wasted your time and are probably becoming even more frustrated about your game. In golf, as in life, you can rarely achieve any goal worth achieving without a little hardwork. There is no such thing as a quick fix and THERE IS NO MAGIC PILL! You have to accept that you **cannot** do the same thing you are used to doing and expect a better result!

But if your body is not ready to make a swing change then you are caught in a round- about scenario. Regardless of how hard you try to change, you will keep falling back to the same incorrect movement that you have been used to making, simply because your body is not ready to move more efficiently!

# Where did it go wrong?

After several years of coaching golf, trying to help students improve, while growing more and more frustrated on their behalf, I realized that the quickest way for them to improve is to go directly to the "root of the problem". The root of almost every golfer's problem lies in their bodies. Even though it is the golfclub that hits the ball, it is your body that swings the golfclub, and what your body CAN or CANNOT do is specific to YOU! Now luckily, most of us are born with a perfectly functional body which means we are born with natural freedom of movement and range of motion.

Now lets take a step back in time to your youth. As a baby we start to learn movement by developing muscles and then learning how to control them in specific movement patterns so if we are stuck lying on our bellies, we can roll over on our backs.

> Now lets take a step back in time to your youth. As a baby we start to learn movement by developing muscles and then learning how to control them in specific movement patterns so if we are stuck lying on our bellies, we can roll over on our backs.

With full range of motion in our joints and as our muscles strengthen we begin to learn how to crawl. Then as we start to play we often do so in a deep squat position, WOW, now that is a difficult position on so many levels!

Then as we develop we eventually learn how to stand and walk and learn to master our movement throughout our lives.

Unfortunately, movement can get limited throughout life too. Injury, repetitive movement, poor posture, and the ageing process are all things that can limit our range of movement. Poor posture is very common amongst the last few generations of the western world. We are raised into a sedentary lifestyle already from when we attend grade school, where we are asked to remain in our seats for hours on end(literally) or else be sent to the detention hall! We sit in our cars as we drive to work, we sit at our office desk all day, then back to our homes to spend a relaxing evening with our familys…on the couch watching the game, or the latest episode of Desperate Housewives!

The aging process is also a very important factor. Studies have shown that with a sedentary lifestyle muscles will diminish about 50% between the ages of 20-50 years old. On top of that the average person will lose an extra 30% of their strength from when they are 50-70 years old. It is not just muscle strength and size that will diminish in the aging process, but study's also show that neural muscular reaction time will also slow down, which means your movement in general will slow down, making it more difficult to perform finite athletic movements such as golf. Finally, our joint mobility and muscles flexibility will also decrease due to increased water content in our soft muscle tissue. Frankly, we lose our body strength and freedom of movement because we stop using it as it was meant to be used. Listen, do you hear that?..... After reading these statistics an alarm clock should be going off in your head convincing you to live an active lifestyle that will help prevent injury and slow down the aging process. And for Pete's sake, stop driving those buggies around the golfcourse! And yes, luckily it is never too late to get back on a pilgrimage to a better body!

# IT is NEVER too late to get started!!

Now that you have gained a better understanding of how going through life, including school, work, lifestyle, and the general ageing process can affect your body, and make it difficult for you to make an efficient golf swing and prevent injuries. You will need to learn how to alter some of the unfortunate side effects that life can bring. You will need to address some of the physical issues with a structured training program that is designed to improving YOUR limitations and the aging process. Unfortunately most golfers will not benefit from doing the regular workouts that are advertised at the local gym. First, you will need to find YOUR strengths and weaknesses, and then develop a program that is designed on improving better movement in your body. In order for your body to have improved movement, you will need to gain better mobility and stability in your joints. Mobility and Stability is the pattern of human joint function that has been extensively researched and understood through the expert eyes of renowned physical therapist Gray Cook[4] and strength and conditioning coach Mike Boyle. Which basically explains how our bodies can move effectively because of the huge roll our joints have when making any specific movement. In order to regain or maintain movement in our joints and strength in our muscles, experts recommend doing a movement related workout frequently. How frequently? Well a good rule of thumb is once a week for every decade you've lived. If you are 70 and retired, that is great, the experts recommend 7 days a week of movement related exercise. Light Yoga or Thai Chi are excellent movement programs for this age group! So what are you waiting for, put down this book and get moving! .....STOP! Hold your hourses, first you need to read a bit further and learn more about YOUR body!

4. Read more at www.greycook.com & www.bodybyboyle.com.

# Stability / Mobility

Our bodies are built in such a way that our joints have specific jobs to do which is either to create stability, or to create mobility.

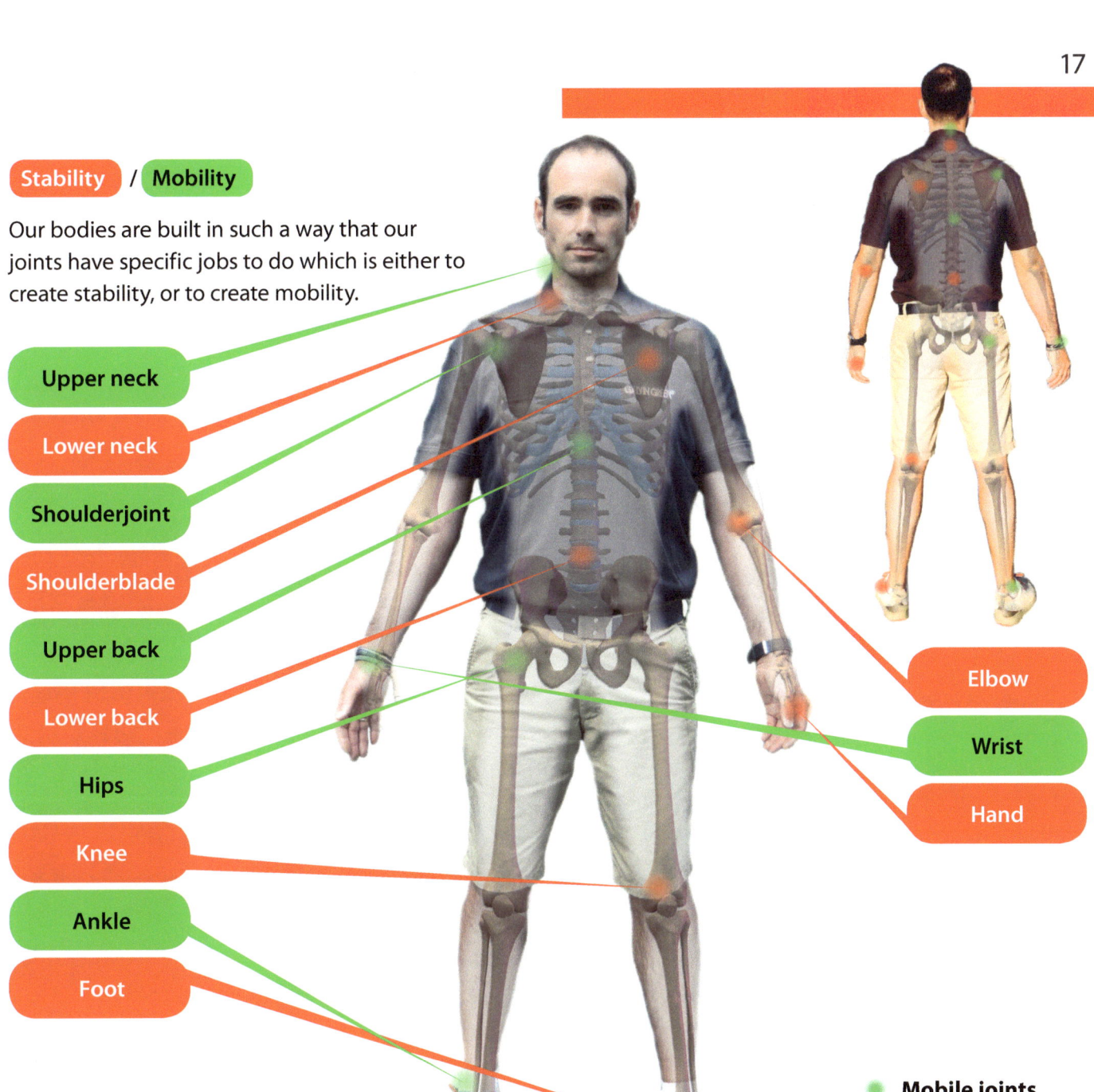

- Upper neck
- Lower neck
- Shoulderjoint
- Shoulderblade
- Upper back
- Lower back
- Hips
- Knee
- Ankle
- Foot
- Elbow
- Wrist
- Hand

● Mobile joints
● Stabile joints

Our joints have a pattern they follow, so that for every mobile joint in the body the next joint in this chain will be a stabile one. Problems first occur if one of our joints is not functioning correctly. This will entail added stress on the next joint in this chain, either above or below the faulty joint. Often causing a negative chain reaction of events in your body.

An example of this would be if our hip, which is a mobile joint, lacks mobility. The hips are one of the most important joints in the body relative to the golf swing. Our hips have rotational components in the backswing and downswing that are imperative when trying to generate and transfer speed in our golf swing. If our muscles and soft tissue surrounding the hip joint are tight and un-pliable, our hips will usually lack mobility, which will limit our ability to make the rotary movement required in an effective golf swing. In an attempt to overcome this lack of mobility, we often learn to compensate for the lack of movement subconsciously, usually by sliding our hips sideways. Not only will this put our lower back(stabile joint) and knee(stabile joint) under enormous stress, but it will also leave our golf swing in a position that lacks power and efficiency. If we are unaware of this, we will continue down this path of self-destruction eventually getting injured. The pain from these injuries is usually NOT in the joint that is faulty(our hip in this case), but instead the joint that gets put under extra stress will suffer, simply because we unconsciously use it to assist the faulty joint in a specific movement…such as golf! Do not take pain lightly. By ignoring it and thinking you can work through it, it will only get worse. Pain is your body's natural warning system, telling you something is wrong. So unless you are interested in chronic pain and permanent injury, listen to yourself and find out how to fix it!

# A body that lacks correct movement in the golf swing is sustainable to injuries!

Our joints have tremendous jobs to do in our daily life and in our golf swings! So in order to prevent injury and maximize our bodies' potential in performing a more effective golf swing that will give us more consistency and improved distance, you'll need to learn more about YOUR body and find out if you have any unwanted limitations!

YOU NEED ONLY 2 TOOLS IN LIFE:

WD-40 & DUCT TAPE

If it doesn't move but should,

USE WD-40.

If it moves and shouldn't,

USE DUCT TAPE @EarlDibblesJr

# How efficient do your joints move?

### Do they move?

- **NO**
  - **SHOULD THEY MOVE?**
    - **NO** → NO PROBLEM!
    - **YES** → FIX IT!
- **YES**
  - **SHOULD THEY MOVE?**
    - **YES** → NO PROBLEM!
    - **NO** → FIX IT!

# 3 Steps to a healthy golf swing:

**1. Learn about YOUR body**

**2. Learn good posture**

**3. Use steps 1 & 2 to learn a healthier more effective golf swing!**

# Chapter 3:
# Know YOUR body! *(The meat and potatoes)*

**YOUR body.... YOUR golf swing!**
So how do you figure out if your body is ready to move efficiently without compensating for unknown limitations? How do you find out how to earn the right to a healthy golf swing?

As you have read earlier on in this book, there are a lot of body parts that need to move efficiently, and there are a lot of reasons to why you might have lost efficient movement in some of these body parts.

The best way to know if your body is ready or if you have problem areas that need improvement, would be to book a screening with a TPI (Titleist performance institute)[5] certified professional. Click on the link at the bottom of this page to find a local expert. The advantages in going to a TPI certified expert is that they have a vast understanding of how the body's muscles and joints work in the golf swing. The physical screening that they will perform on you will help evaluate both your strengths and weaknesses in your body and how they relate to your golf swing. After you have been screened by a TPI expert, they will also assist you by giving you a program that will help you on the right track to improvement and measurable results! Usually programs will consist of simple exercises that can be performed at home for a few minutes a day. Normally you will see improvements within 4-6 weeks of performing these exercises. Then all of a sudden, ALACAZAM you are on your way to a better golf swing and on the right path to improvement and success!

It would be a good idea to book a visit with your expert again after 6 weeks to make sure your still on the right

path, and perhaps move on to more advanced exercises that will lead to even better results. I would also recommend you using a training notebook to record your steady progress of improvement, in order to give yourself new goals to continue your body's improvement.

**Self-screening**
If you do not have a TPI expert in your area, I have developed a physical screening test in the following chapter that you can take in the company of a partner to assist in evaluating the quality of your movements. When taking this screening on your own, it is very important, that you never let that little voice in your head take over trying to impress yourself or your helper. Do not let your ultra ego get in your way. This test is designed to check where you limitations are, not push you beyond them. If you push yourself during the screening there is a possibility that you could provoke an injury that might be on the verge of occurring but could have been avoided if the correct exercises were applied first. So be sure to test yourself using common sense, improvement will come shortly down the road!

5. Read more about TPI and find a TPI-certificeret expert in your area at www.myTPI.com.

# Self-screening

**IMPORTANT! (use the screeningsheet found at the end of this chapter to record test results)**

If any pain or discomfort is felt during the tests STOP immediately!

When taking these tests there is NO grey area. You either can or you cannot do the test correctly, there are no points for almost! By giving yourself a pass because you can almost do an exercise, you are only robbing yourself from a more efficient golf swing!

This test is not meant to be taken alone, so call a friend that can assist and spot you when doing it. Or better yet, take the test with another golf enthusiast who will also benefit from the test. That way you will be able to assist each other under the screening process while at the same time encouraging and helping each other to stay motivated. By surrounding yourself with people that share your interest for improving, you are creating the perfect environment for self-growth!

# Test 1: Pelvic tilt

This test is intended to check your pevlic mobility. Your pelvis is the joining segment of your body that attaches your lower and upper body together and plays a huge part in how efficiently your body can move.

Stand in your golf posture and cross your arms so that your hands are placed on the opposite shoulders.

WITHOUT changing your posture, try and arch your lower back and then tuck it under. Repeat a few times and check for loss of posture in the upper spine as well as how efficiently your pelvis can move back and forth. If there is limited movement in one or both directions make note. Then use the corrective exercises on the opposite page to improve your pelvic mobility. If there is reasonable range of movement but shaking occurs as you tuck your pelvis under, you have strength issues in your core muscles. See the exercises for test 9, which are also targeted at strengthening the pelvic region.

# Exercises

## Cats & Dogs

Begin this exercise down on all fours with your hands directly under your shoulders and your knees under your hips. Now without bending your elbows, arch your back like a dog and then round your back like a cat. Repeat this exercise three times. Then try to find a neutral position where your lower back is flat. Breath deeply filling your abdomen with air three times. With every exhall tighten your abdominal muscles. Repeat 10 times.

## Supine pelvic tilts to neutral

Lay on your back with your knees bend and your feet flat on the floor. Now alternate between arching and flattening your lower back - trying not to move your upper body too much. Then find a neutral position and breath deeply filling your abdomen with air three times. With every exhale tighten your abdominal muscles. Repeat 10 times.

# Test 2: Pelvic rotation

In this test we are checking to see if your upper body has the ability to move freely from your lower body. This is an extremely important part of how the body can generate elastic energy and power in the golf swing, which is potentially the most important factor to increasing clubhead speed i.e. for **more distance!**

Take your golf posture and cross your arms so that your hands are resting on opposite shoulders. Now focus on rotating your hips while your shoulders stay still. See how smoothly your hips can rotate in both directions. If your hips move more laterally from side to side, this may indicate that you have limitations! If you have poor rotation issues, have your spotter stabilize you by grabbing a hold of your shoulders then try again. If this helps, you may have stability issues. Lack of mobility or stability in pelvic rotation will lead to inefficiency's in your golf swing. This is a serious RED flag that needs to be taken care of.

# Exercise

### Stork turns

Standing on one leg you can use a golfclub or place your hands flat on a wall to help maintain balance. If you have good balance try without support by crossing your arms and placing your hands on the opposite shoulders. Now lift one foot and tuck it in behind the knee of the supporting leg. Now drive your raised knee over the supporting leg moving it back and forth while maintaining a steady upper body.

Do this exercise 10 times on each leg.

# Test 3: Hip Rotation

This test checks your ankle and hips ability to rotate internally and externally in the golf swing. The lack of ability to rotate in these two joints during the golf swing leads to some of the most criminal yet most common swing faults that are out there. This is potentially the leading cause of injuries such as back pain.

Take a two irons and place them on the floor in the form of an X. Now stand on one foot pointing it towards the middle of the "X"(45degrees), while the toe of the other foot is on the ground approximatly one foot behind the lead foot . Now place your hands on your hips and turn them in both directions. Have your spotter check if you are able to turn a full 60 degrees while making sure your supporting foot stays flat on the floor. This means that you will need to turn a full 15 degrees past the shaft your hip is turning towards. Now change legs and try the otherside.

# Exercise

## Clamshells
Lie down on your side with your knees bend and your feet on top of each other. Keep your feet together and elevate your top knee as much as possible.
Repeat 10 times then change sides and repeat.

## Foam roller
Sit on a firm foam roller horizontally so you are resting on your hip. Now, roll slowly up and down five times then alter leg positions to reach different areas of the muscles and soft muscle tissue that need to be loosened up.
Change sides and repeat.

## Hip circles
Stand on all fours then with a neutral spine and tighten your abdominal muscles up. Lift your left leg to the side maintaining the flex in your knee. Now move your left leg in large circular motion without jeopardizing the stability in your back. Repeat 10 times on both sides.

# Test 4: Toe touch

This is a great test to check your mobility in your hips, mid-back as well as hamstrings. It is crucial to have this ability when trying to maintain a good posture throughout your golf swing. Stand tall with your arms straight over your head, your feet together and knees straight. Now while maintaining straight knees, push your butt back then bend over forward and try to touch your toes. If you cannot touch your toes, then place one of your feet back and elevate the heel so that that leg is slightly bend. At the same time keeping your supporting leg straight. Now try again. Change legs and repeat. If one side is easier than the other there might only be an issue with the one side, get it fixed!

# Exercise

## Heaven to earth

Elevate your toes up on a telephone book, a case of Titleist balls, or something of similar height. Now roll a towel together and pinch it between your knees. Stretch your hands up towards heaven then slowly bend forwards and reach down to the earth. Repeat 10 times.

Now repeat this exercise, but instead of elevating your toes, elevate your heels.

# Test 5: Deep squat

An efficient golf swing generates power from the ground up through the entire body, which in turn helps maximize club head speed, solid contact, and injury prevention. Studies have proven that there is a direct correlation between your body's ability to do a deep squat and how efficiently your body can utilize and transfer the power generated from the ground up in your golf swing.

Now stand with your feet shoulders width apart and your toes pointing forward. Take a shaft and hold it above your head with your elbows bend at 90 degrees. Raise your arms up so that the shaft is behind your head. Now sink down into a deep squat trying to maintain the shaft behind your head and your heels in contact with the ground. Your knees should be pointing straight forward as your butt reaches knee height. If you have failed to do this then try again, but this time without the shaft, placeing your thumbs on your collarbone.

If you feel any discomfort or pain while attempting these tests, stop immediately!

# Exercise

### Deep squat straight arms assisted heels
Elevate your heels up on the edge of a telephone book. Now attempt doing the squat again as described on page 36. If this is still causing difficulties, try without the shaft up over your head. Come down into the bottom of the deep squat, reach out with one arm in front of you and elevate that arm up and behind, then alternate arms. Repeat this exercise 10 times with each arm. Then try 10 times with the shaft up above your head.

### Deep squat assisted with weight
In this exercise you should use a 5 to 10kg weight to start out with. You can also use a backpack full of books or improvise with what you have got around you. Then you will need a chair or table that approximatly reachs knee height. At first try elevating your heels under a telephone book and then progress to flat feet on the ground. Start by holding the weight with straight arms in front of you, then slowly descend into a deep squat. Place the weight on the chair and let go of it. Stay down in position for 10 seconds before rising up out of it.
Repeat 10 times.

### Goblet squat
Stand with your feet shoulder width apart and toes pointing straight forward. Place the weight at your chest with both hands. Descend into a deep squat position while keeping your elbows in between your knees, and your head and chest up. Repeat 10 times!

# Test 6: Lats

In this test we are checking your shoulder mobility as well as the flexibilty of the long back muscles. Lack of flexibility in this area can translate into loss of posture in your golf swing as well as lack of efficiency when transferring power from one body segment to the next.
Lie down on your back with your knees bend and feet flat on the ground. Now your head, shoulder blades and lower back need to stay in contact with the floor.

Stretch your arms out along your sides with your thumbs pointing up. Lift your arms up and keep them straight while extending them behind your head and try to reach the floor. If your lower back starts to arch, losing contact with the floor, make a note of where the arms are at that point.

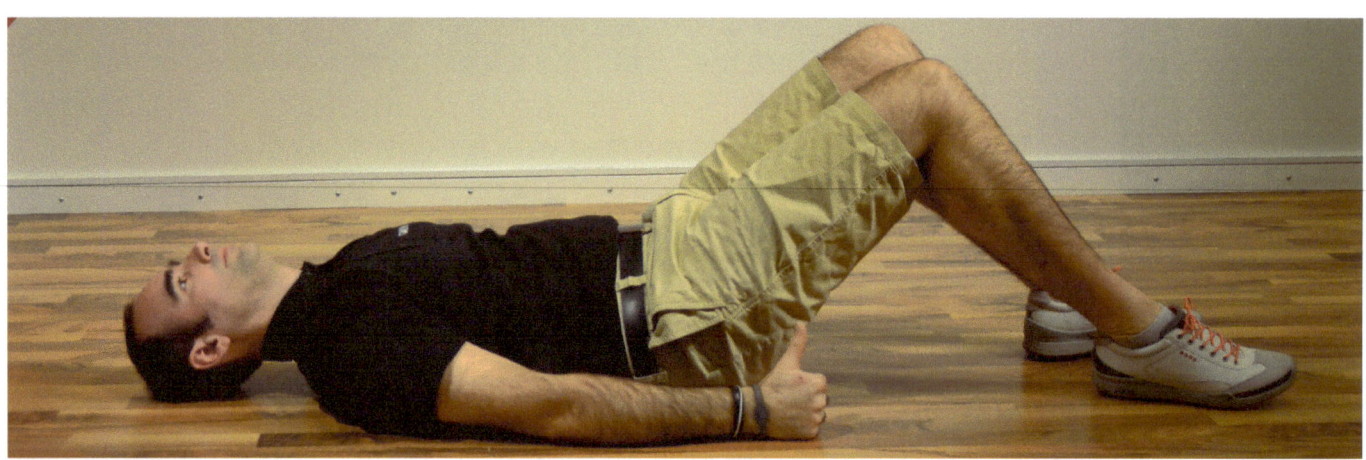

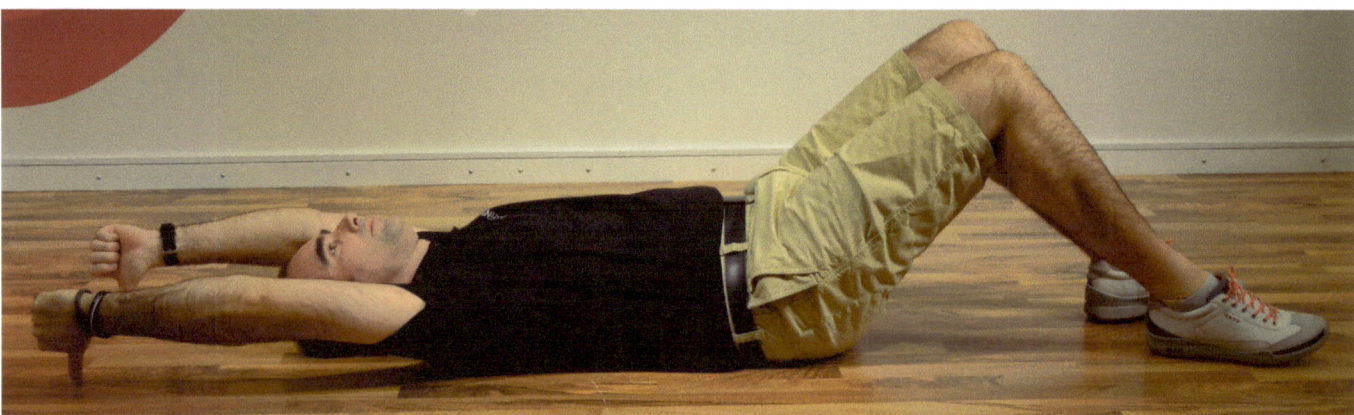

# Exercise

### Sitting prayer
Come down on the floor and sit on your heels. Now place both your hands on a palates ball in front of you. While maintaining contact with your hands on the ball and your butt on your heels, roll the ball forward so that your head falls down between your arms. Stay down in this position for three deep breathes, trying to focus on getting the air deep into your abdominal area. Now slowly roll the ball to one side and hold it for a few seconds, then to the other side.

### Foam roller
Lie with the side of your chest on a firm foam roller. Now slowly roll up and down the side of your chest five times. Alternate sides and repeat.

# Test 7: Single leg balance

This test is to check how well you can maintain your balance. Balance is crucial in your golf swing when trying to make a swing with any kind of efficiency.
Lift one knee up to waist height and let your arms hang at your sides. When you are in balance close your eyes and start to count. Repeat on the other leg.

**0-5 seconds:**
You need some extremely wide shoes!

**6-10 seconds:**
Not great

**11-15 seconds:**
Not bad, but with room for improvement!

**16-20 seconds:**
Good

**More than 21 seconds:**
PGA Tour-standard

# Exercise

### Ankle windshield wipers

Sit on a bar stole, make two fists with your hands and place them together between your knees. Now press your knees into your fists and roll your ankles from side to side like windshield wipers.

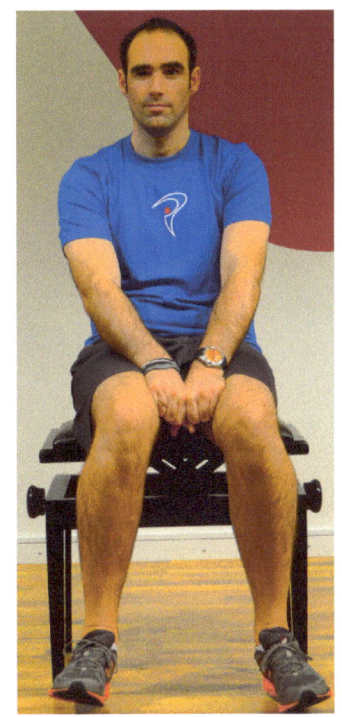
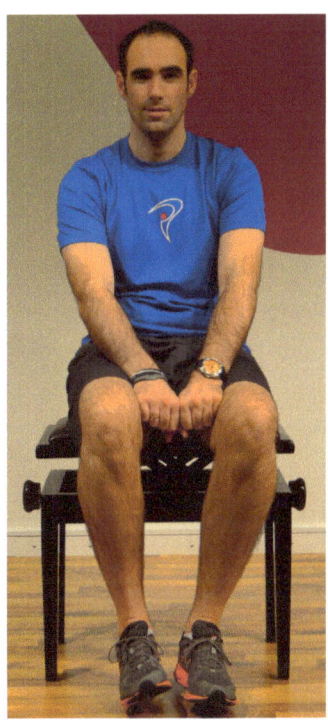

### Beware of the blind, one-legged golfer!

Standing in your golf posture kick one foot out behind you at knee height. Now make little swings from side to side. try to continue for 20 seconds then repeat on the other leg. When this exercise seems easy, then try it with closed eyes.

# Test 8: Seated rotation

This test checks your upper backs ability to rotate. In the golf swing this can be one of the main causes of lose of posture, back injuries, and also lack of power.

Use two shafts to make an "X" in a 90 degree angle and place a chair so it is pointing towards the middle of the cross. Sit with your butt at the edge of the chair and with your knees and feet together. Now hold a shaft up across your shoulders, keep your knees together and turn your shoulders as far as you can to one side, then repeat to the other side. Keep your knees still and make sure that it is your upper body that turns and not just your shoulder girdles.

To pass this test you should be able to turn your shoulders 45-degrees to each side.

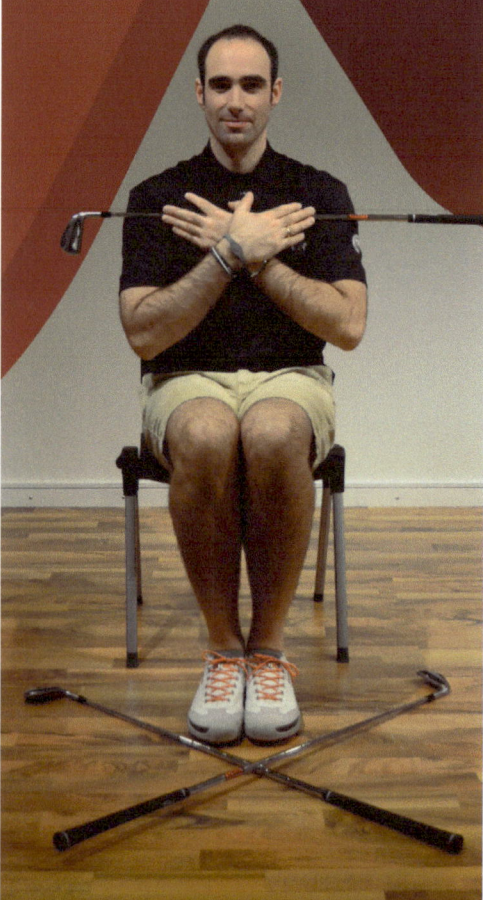
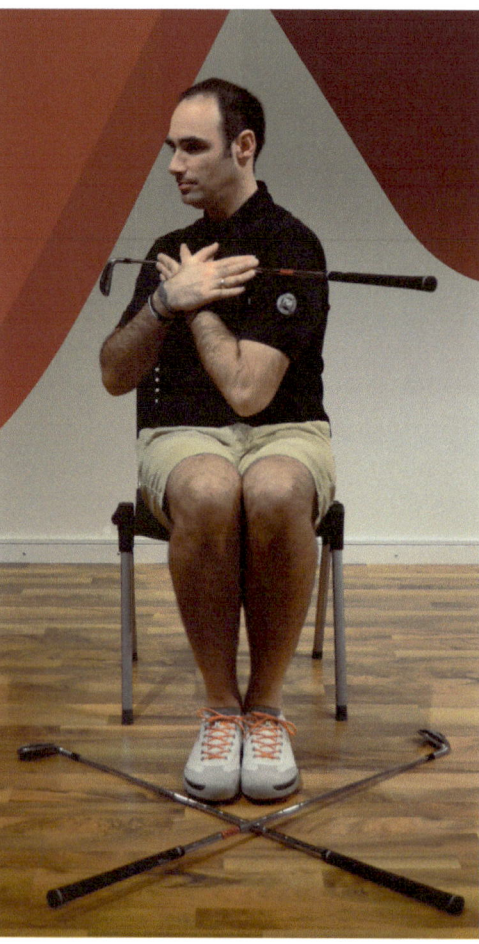

# Exercise

### Open books cages
Lie down on one side with your upper knee placed on the ground in front of you. Now take your hand from your lower arm and lock your upper knee to the ground. Place your upper hand on the floor in front of you, then lift it up and stretch it behind you. Repeat 10 times then move on to your otherside and repeat.

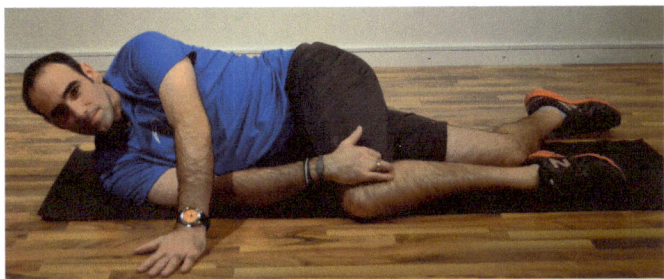

### Half kneeling long turns
Stand tall on one knee, push your pelvis forward and tighten your butt muscles. Place a shaft across your shoulders. While maintaining your height and core stability turn your chest towards your forward leg. Repeat 10 times and change to the other leg.

# Test 9: Core stability

This test checks how good you are at activating your butt muscles. In the golf swing we often use the saying that the "core is the king". Well, your core is the name we give to the muscles that stabilize the mid-section of our body, and out of those muscles the butt muscles are the king, so you do the math, important? Oh yeah! Lie down on your back and bend your knees so that your feet are flat on the ground. Extend your arms up over head with palms together. Now lift your butt up and extend your hip so that your thighs and your back are in a straight line. Now straighten one leg out in extension of your straight body and hold for 12 seconds. Come down and relax for a second then up again and repeat with your other leg.

If your butt starts to fall down or starts to move slightly to one side, or if your leg starts to cramp then this would be a fail. But don't worry, a fail would be great news, because just think of how vast your improvements in your golf swing will be when you learn to activate your King of Kings correctly! This is literally awesome!

# Exercise

## Butt lifts

Lie down on your back and bend your knees so that your feet are flat on the ground. Place a folded towel between your knees and start with your arms at your side. Now lift your butt up and at the same time lift your arms up over your head. While pinching the towel between your knees try to get your butt up high so that your thighs and chest are in a straight line.
Repeat 10 times

## Bird dogs with extension

Come down on all fours. Find a neutral position where your lower back is flat. Now tighten your abdominal muscles and lift your left leg and right arm up at the same time. Point your right thumb up into the air and keep your abdominal muscles tight. Be careful not to arch your back while doing this exercise as the goal is to have your butt muscles do the lifting, not your lower back. Repeat 10 times on each side.

# Test 10: Shoulder rotation

The object of the 90/90 test is to check your shoulder mobility and scapular stability. Lack of strength and flexibility in the shoulders will make it difficult to transfer energy from your body to your arms in the golf swing.

Standing tall, straightening one arm out to the side, bend your elbow until your forearm reaches a 90-degree angle facing forward. Now, while maintaining your elbow at shoulder height rotate your arm up and as far back as you can.

Measure how far your forearm can rotate in relation to your upper spine. Change sides and try again.

Now repeat the test from your golf posture to check for shoulder stability.
Make a note if the results are the same as, less than or greater than standing.

# Exercise

### Angel wings
Stand in your golfposture holding a light weight in each hand(example water bottles).
Now lift your arms like you are spreading your wings, while still remaining in your golfposture. Repeat 10 times.

### Saturday Night Fever
Stand in your golf posture holding a light weight in each hand (example a water bottle).
Lift one arm and rotate it behind you, then as you return the arm back down infront of you lift the other arm so that you are alternating between the two. Repeat 10 times with each arm.

# How to use this screening

I suggest making a photocopy of the screen sheet so that you can use the original for the rescreening in 6 weeks time. Under each of the tests you can indicate by circling off your test result. The green areas are Green flags indicating that you are fine in that area. The red areas are RED FLAGS indicating that improvement is necessary in these areas. Red flag areas need to be fixed to prevent your body from making compensations in your golf swing that will potentially cause injuries, and a less effective golf swing!

## NEVER IGNORE RED FLAGS!

# Screening-sheet

Date: _____  Name: _____

## 1. Pelvic tilt

| Good | Limited arching | Limited flattening | Both are limited |
|---|---|---|---|
| | | | |

| Good smooth movement | Not smooth or shaky |
|---|---|
| | |

## 2. Pelvic rotation

| Good rotational movement | Limited rotation, more lateral slide |
|---|---|
| | |

| Improves with hold | doesn't improve with hold |
|---|---|
| | |

## 3. Lower body rotation

| Left side | | More than 60 degrees | 60 degrees | Less than 60 degrees |
|---|---|---|---|---|
| Turn Right | Turn left | RT      LT | RT      LT | RT      LT |
| Right side | | More than 60 degrees | 60 degrees | Less than 60 degrees |
| Turn Right | Turn left | RT      LT | RT      LT | RT      LT |

## 4. Toe touch

| Can | Can't touch | Left side can't touch | Right side can't touch |
|---|---|---|---|
| | | | |

## 5. Deep squat

| Arms stay behind head | Arms come infront of head | Arms down limited |
|---|---|---|
| | | |

6. Inspired by myTPI.com

## 6. Lats

| Can touch floor | Arms reach between nose and floor | Above nose |
|---|---|---|
| | | |

## 7. Single leg balance

| Right leg | 0-5 sec. | 6-10 sec. | 11-15 sec. | 16-20 sec. | More than 21 sec. |
|---|---|---|---|---|---|
| | | | | | |
| Left leg | 0-5 sec. | 6-10 sec. | 11-15 sec. | 16-20 sec. | More than 21 sec. |
| | | | | | |

## 8. Seated Trunk rotation

| Left side | More than 45 degrees | 45 degrees | Less than 45 Degrees |
|---|---|---|---|
| | | | |
| Right side | More than 45 Degrees | 45 Degrees | Less than 45 Degrees |
| | | | |

## 9. Core stability

| Right side | Strength normal | Strength weak | Cramping |
|---|---|---|---|
| | | | |
| Left side | Strength normal | Strength weak | Cramping |
| | | | |

## 10. Shoulder mobility/stability

| Standing | | Greater than spine angle | | Equal to spine angle | | Less than spine angle | |
|---|---|---|---|---|---|---|---|
| Right side | Left side | RT | LT | RT | LT | RT | LT |
| Golfposture | | Greater than standing | | Equal to standing | | Less than standing | |
| | | | | | | | |

7. Inspired by myTPI.com

# Chapter 4:
# Unlocking YOUR Golf swing's Potential!

# Unlocking your golf swings potential!

As you have learned so far, and hopefully grasped, the secret ingredient to an efficient golf swing is a well functioning body. And understanding YOUR body is the key to unlocking YOUR golf swings potential. Finding your limitations and improving them is how you will EARN the right to improvement. However, sometimes improving your limitations will leave you in unchartered waters! You may need to re-learn a few basic things about your posture before you can swing a golf club efficiently. There are two major areas that bad posture affects our golf swing. The first is when our shoulders round too far forward when standing in golf posture. The second is when there is too much arching in the lower back in our golf posture. Both of these postures are incredibly destructive when trying to create an efficient and athletic golf swing because they will limit the freedom of movement that our mobile joints such as our hips and upper back should have.

# Poor posture = Red flags!

Which as we now know will leave added stress on our stabile joints such as our lower back for example causing our body to move with poor efficiency that can result in injury!

Bad posture in these two areas can be due to muscle imbalances called upper-cross-syndrome and lower-cross-syndrome. Upper and lower-cross-syndrome is a condition made aware to the professional world by Dr. Vladimir Janda[8]. To simplify, if you have rounded shoulders when taking your golf posture, you basically have tight upperback/neck muscles and weakened mid back muscles, combined with tight chest muscles and weak front neck flexors.

If your lower back is too arched when standing in your golf posture, you basically have tight lower back muscles and tight muscles through your pelvis and on the front of your hips(hip flexors), contra weak abdominal and butt muscles.

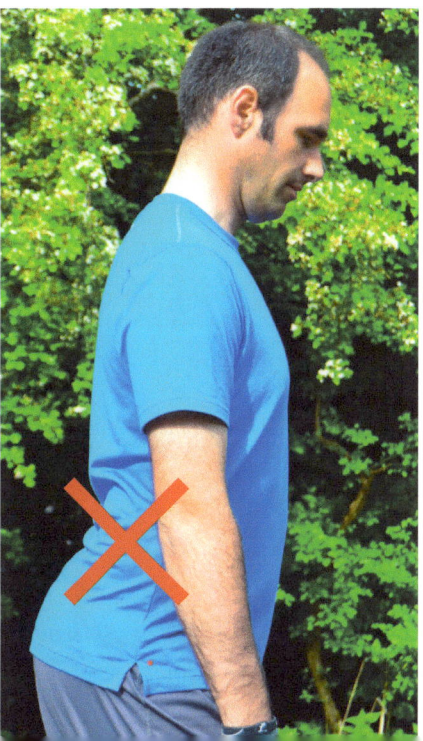

8. read more on www.jandaapproach.com

# How is your posture?

Here is how you can check to see if you have poor posture. Simply have a friend take a picture of you from the side as you take your stance and address the ball. Make sure that they take the picture directly down the line from the hand position so that there is a good angle to see your whole back from the tailbone up to the neck. Now check if you have rounded shoulders that slump forward or an arched lower back. Both are very common but very destructive for you and your golf swing!

## Typical swing faults caused by poor posture

# C-Posture

If your shoulders are rounded forward you have C-posture and possibly upper cross syndrome. This position will put huge limitations on your ability to turn your body correctly during your golf swing, often forcing you to stand up out of your posture in order to make a backswing!

# Corrective exercises for C-Posture

Stand tall on one knee, push your pelvis forward and tighten your butt muscles. Place a shaft across your shoulders and while maintaining your height and core stability turn your chest towards your forward bend leg. Repeat 10 times then change to the other leg.

### Foam rolling
Lie down with the foam roller under your upper back, and then slowly roll up and down from the top of your back to mid back. Elevate your butt off the ground and let your own body weight press into your upper back muscles.

Here is a great exercise to stretch your pec. minor muscle. Stand in a door way and place your arm up against the door well. Turn away with your body so that you feel a really good stretch in your upper chest. Hold for 10 sec. then alternate to the other side.

Pectoralis minor is a small muscle that is on the top of your chest. When it is tight it will shorten pulling your shoulders forward and cause "C" posture. Here is a great exercise to stretch it out again.

# S-Posture

If your lower back is too arched you have S-posture and possible lower cross syndrome. Having S-posture means that your golf swings motor is turned off! Your abdominal and butt muscles or better known as your "core" muscles are shut off when standing in S posture, and in the golf swing the core is the king!

# Corrective exercises for S-Posture

Begin this exercise down on all fours with your hands directly under your shoulders and your knees under your hips. Now without bending your elbows, arch your back like a dog and then round your back like a cat. Repeat this exercise three times then try to find a neutral position where your lower back is flat. Take three deep breaths filling your abdomen like a balloon and then with every exhale tighten your abdominal muscles. Repeat 10 times.

**Half kneeling long turns**
Stand tall on one knee, push your pelvis forward and tighten your butt muscles to feel a stretch along the front side of the leg that is placed on the ground. Place a shaft across your shoulders and while maintianing your height and core stability turn your chest towards your front leg. Repeat 10 times then change to the other leg.

**Bird dog extensions**
Come down on the floor on all fours. Find a neutral position where your lower back is flat. Now tighten your abdominal muscles and lift your left leg and right arm up at the same time. Point your right thumb up in the air while maintaining your abdominal muscles tight. Be careful not to arch your back while doing this exercise as the goal is to have your butt muscles do the lifting, not your lower back. Repeat 10 times on each side.

"If you have a body – you are an athlete"
Bill Bowermann

## Chapter 5:
# Great body... great golf swing

**Great body = Great Athlete = Great golf swing!**
So far you have been screened for limitations and are either working on improving them or you are good to go! This means your body is earning the right to a better golf swing, awesome right? Wait a minute….put those arms down, it is not time to celebrate quite yet! Having a fully functional body is #1 in golf, but we also need to learn an efficient movement.

Once again, booking a lesson with an experienced PGA professional will now come in handy, because now we need to teach your body how to control all its newly added range of motion!

In order to utilize your body's full potential in your golf swing you will have to:
- Have a functional body with good mobility / stability
- Have good posture
- Learn an effective athletic movement

# How it all works!

In all great athletic movements the body needs to move efficiently to create power and speed. And golf is no different, from the moment you begin your backswing, your body will begin working. Similar to a slingshot, your body must have mobility so that when you turn in your backswing the different muscles will begin to stretch like the elastic on the slingshot.

But you also need stability in the stabile joints, similar to the handle on the slingshot. The slingshot analogy explains how your body stores elastic energy in the backswing, which gives you a ton of potential energy to deliver to the ball when done correctly.

9. Slingshot analogy from Jason Glass, learn more at http://www.jasonglassperformancelab.com

However, potential energy does not equal power unless it gets released correctly! So how do you release this stored potential energy correctly? In order to release all this stored energy that is stretched in your body like the elastic on the slingshot, you will need to start your downswing in a specific order.

In fact, the best players in the world not only create elastic energy in their backswings, they increase that elastic stretch in their downswings before releasing it so they can deliver maximum speed to the clubhead.

Imagine you are holding the handle of the slingshot with your left hand and pulling the elastic with your right. But just before you release the elastic with your right hand, you move the handle with your left hand further away creating an extra stretch in the elastic and then...wait for it.... KAAPOWW you release the elastic on the slingshot with your right hand! Now that is how the best players in the world create explosive power!

**Elastic energy**

**Increased elastic energy = KAPOW'r!**

Similar to throwing a ball. In order to throw the ball efficiently, your body and throwing arm start by moving in opposite directions so that your body and weight is moving forward and turning while your throwing arm and wrist are moving backwards reating a stretch throughout your body. Then KA-POW, your forward moving and turning body pulls your throwing arm forward to catapult the ball with maximum speed and accuracy in the direction you want to throw it. Now stand up and give it a try. Do you feel the stretch, do you feel the kapow'r?

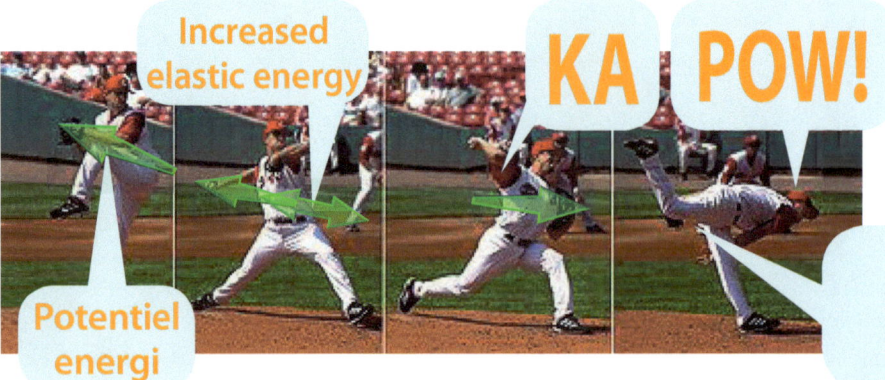

**Potentiel energi**

**Increased elastic energy**

**KA POW!**

**Energy released**

So how does all this work in the golf swing? Let us start by dividing your body into three parts:
- Pelvis/hips
- Chest/shoulders
- Arms/hands/club

In your backswing you are turning your body away from your target, creating a stretch from the ground up. Your legs and hips are stabile but turning as your upper body turns further while maintaining its forward posture, creating a slight stretch. Just before the arms/hands/club reach the top of the backswing, your hips are already firing and moving forward while turning, creating a larger stretch between your hips and chest. And then, just like the baseball pitcher, the javelin thrower, or an ATHLETE, ...KAPOW'r!

This is a huge key to how you can add extra length to your game. Not only will you increase your distance, but your direction and consistency will also improve dramatically. You see, by earning the right to an efficient athletic golf swing, your body can learn to swing more athletically, naturally and with more efficiency, as it was meant to move, as you were born to move! And that is what the golf swing is all about!

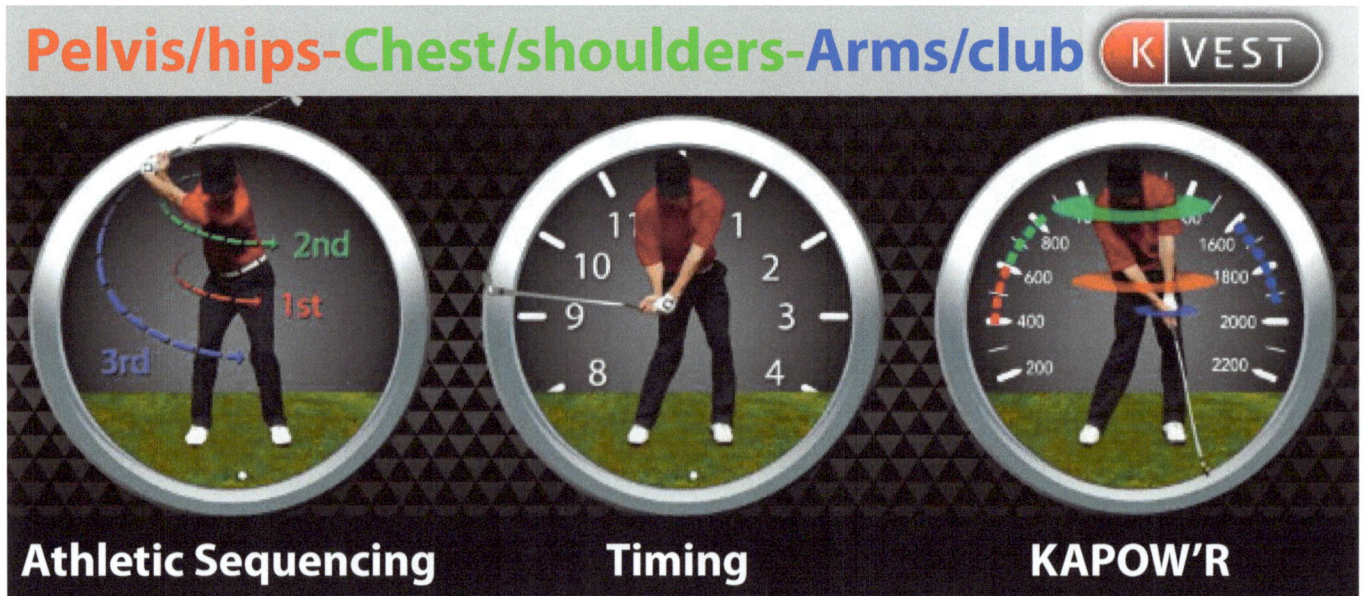

Read more at www.k-vest.com

# Swing drills to improve athletic sequence

## Swing drill #1

Place the ball on a low tee. Now stand with your feet together though behind the ball. As you start swinging the club back, start moving your lead leg simultaneously towards the target. As you plant your lead foot on the ground you should have reached the top of your backswing and be able to feel a stretch from your lead hip up to your trail shoulder. Now finish your golf swing. This drill is excellent for teaching your body the correct athletic sequence in the golf swing where your lower body starts the downswing.

## Swing drill # 2

As you swing back lift your lead heel. This will allow you to turn more freely in your backswing. Though, be careful NOT to rise up and out of your posture. Now start your downswing by planting your lead heel hard down on the ground again. Starting your downswing with your lead heel is a fantastic way to creat correct athletic sequencing by getting your weight to shift back onto your lead side and help rotate your body back towards the target creating rotational power. Finish your swing in balance with your weight in your lead heel and the trail toe!

## Swing drill # 3

Stand at the front and slightly to the side of a golf buggy and place your club head on the tire(which should be in the middle of your stance). Now take a swing returning the clubhead back to the tire. Now put some sugar in it, really leaning your weight into the tire creating some serious pressure!

You should feel your hips rotating and your core engaged with your hands slightly ahead of the clubhead, now that's power! Repeat 10 times then see if you can repeat the same feeling on the driving range, alternating back and forth from the tire and hitting the golf balls on the range!

# Chapter 6:
# Get your motor started!

How often do you prepare your body before a round? Perhaps you are now thinking back to a time when you raced out to the first tee without warming up and played one of your best rounds of golf. Well that is all fine and dandy, because I have heard it all before. You may get lucky once or twice but the fact is that to make an athletic movement such as a golf swing your body needs to fine tune its firing system in order to time the correct sequence of movement through your central nervous system. This means your joints need to be mobile, your nervous system needs to be ready to fire quickly and your muscles need to work and relax in the correct order to be able to time a magnificent athletic movement such as a golf swing correctly. These physical demands cannot be fulfilled with a couple of practice swings on the first tee. Your body needs a functional warm-up to be prepared to perform correctly and to prevent risk of injury.

# Functional warm-up

So what is a functional warm-up? We often think of warming up as stretching exercises and flexibility is definately part of it. But a functional warm-up is a lot more than that. The goal of a functional warm-up is to increase your body's range of motion, prepare your central nervous system to fire rapidly in the correct sequence, and to prepare your muscles to work correctly. In the next few pages you will find some of the most important exercises that are designed to help get your motor fired up and ready to perform.

The following exercises should be a deliberate part of your golf round, training or fitness program.

## Warm-up: Foam rolling

These exercises can be done at home or in your hotel room before your round. Rolling on a firm foam roller is a fantastic way to give your muscles and joints a deep massage, which can help loosen you up and give your body a greater range of motion. Roll back and forth on these areas of your body slowly five times. If you find a tight spot stay on it for a few seconds longer. Using a foam roller on a daily basis over stiff areas on the body can reap fantastic effects and longterm results!

## Dynamic warm-up exercise# 1

Hold a golfclub in your left hand, with the buttend on the ground for support. Now push your pelvis forward and tighten your abdominal muscles. Now swing your left leg back and forth while maintaining height with your chest. Make 10 swings forward with the left leg then continue with the side swings below.

Continue with the left leg, but instead of swing back and forth, swing your left leg from side to side with your toe pointing upwards in both directions. Make 10 swings to each side.

Shift to holding the club with your right hand and repeat the same exercise with your right leg.

## Exercise# 2

Stand up tall with a wide stance between your feet. Hold a golfclub out in infront of you with your hands separated at shoulders width. Pull your shoulder blades together so that your chest comes forward; now slowly turn your upper body from side to side while keeping your hips facing forward. Repeat 10 times to each side.

## Exercise# 3

With the same start position as above, this time start rotating your hips in the direction you swing the club. Turn your hips as far as you can without your upperbody/shaft following. Then when you feel your hips can't turn anymore, let them pull your upper body and shaft around so you end up with both your hips and chest facing the target. Make sure your weight ends on your lead side and end standing on your trail foots toe.

## Exercise# 4

Start by standing tall with your feet together. Now take a step forward with your right foot and come down until your right thigh is parallel to the ground. At the same time rotate your upper body to your right side lifting your left arm in the air and letting your right arm point down towards your left heel.

Now return to the start position and repeat with the opposite side. Do eight lunges on each side.

## Exercise# 5

This exercise requires the same start position as above, but when you lunge forward with your right leg rotate your upper body to the left, with your left arm up in the air, and your right arm pointing down at the instep of your right foot. Make sure your trail leg is straight and hold for five seconds then return to start position and alternate to the other side. Repeat five times on each side.

## Exercise# 6

Stand tall with your feet together while holding a golf club out infront of you at chest height. Now lunge forward with your right leg and rotate your upper body to the right. Tighten your butt muscles as you turn and maintain an upright posture with your upper body. Return to start position and alternate to the other side. Repeat five times on each side.

# Chapter 7:
# Nutrition and Energy

Your body is now firing on all cylinders, like a powerful V8 motor it is strong, agile, and fast! Your motor is tuned and ready for action. However you still need to fill your motor with the correct fuel if you want it to perform efficiently. Similarly to if you fueled a diesel motor with gasoline, it will not matter how top tuned your motor is, it will still break down! So even a physically and mentally fit golfer will not make it to the top of the leaderboard without using the correct fuel to maitain a high level of energy. Therefore i have decided to team up with Nutritional Expert Pernille H. Steenberg in the next chapter. Her expertise will leave you with great tips on how you can maintain a healthy level of energy so you can perform at your best on and off the golf course!

## About Pernille

Pernille is a nutritional coach who specializes in time management. She is a FM(Functional medicin)Nutritional Expert and a certified Systematic Coach. On top of that she has over 20 years of experience in the field of strength and conditioning coaching. Pernille reaches many athletes with her "down to earth" approach to health. She specializes in helping everyday people, in all age groups, with busy lifestyles learn how to bring eating right and functional training back into their daily routine.

*"We expect so much of ourselves today. Living up to these expectations - and gaining the most of life - requires a solid base form and a keen sense of the body."*

http://www.pernillehsteenberg.dk

# Your health is YOUR responsibility!

Everybody deserves a healthy lifestyle. Especially with all the benefits there are to gain from living healthy. Healthy people are generally happier, they have more confidence, they are physically and mentally stronger, they are more energetic, and have fewer sick days that can leave them stuck at home! Also healthy people have more positive energy to take on all the challenges that living an ambitious and goal-oriented lifestyle can demand. By understanding your body's basic needs - what fuels you and fills you with energy - you can improve both your quality of life on and off the golf-course! The five most important factors when living a healthy lifestyle are:

**1. Thoughts and feelings 2. Sleep and relaxation 3. Functional movement and training 4. Stress/balance, 5. Nutrition**

Now if you take a closer look at your lifestyle, is there one of these areas that you can improve, so that you can improve your health and your quality of life, and without a doubt also your performance? Maybe you have not been sleeping well lately, or perhaps your work has been demanding extra ordinary efforts that has been taking its toll, or maybe vegetables have had a low priority in your diet, or maybe something totally different that only you can feel. As time goes by these demands might have led to lack of concentration, muscles feeling drained and tight or you just feel like you have not got the same zapp of energy that you are used to. The good news is that you can take charge of your life and that you and only you alone can make a decision to make a change! You can eat, sleep, and train yourself to the healthier lifestyle you want.

Your body is extremely thankful every time you reward it with the attention it needs to feel good!

In this chapter I will help you take charge and understand the importance of living a healthy lifestyle and the effect it will have on your performance on the golf course. You will learn about recovery, hydration, and nutrition. You will only need to improve on one of these areas at a time - though perferably the area that you feel you need the most improvement on. You see, by improving on only one of these areas, you will feel an accomplishment, filling up your Motivations-Motor with positive fuel, which in turn will help you stay motivated to continue to the next area of improvement. If you set your priority on getting a good night sleep, you will wake up feeling fresh with plenty of energy to make a healthy breakfast to start your day off in the right way. Remember, a healthy lifestyle is a journey, not a destination!

# How to maintain Hydration

Being hydrated is one of the basic fundaments of staying alive - this is common knowledge. But after many hours on the golf course, there is a good chance that you have become dehydrated, especially on hot days. The hard facts are that by depleting your body's hydration by only 2% under its normal levels, your energy, your bloodsugar, and your general well being will seriously be effected. Luckily, hydration is easy to maintain. All you have to do is drink water, before, during, and after your round of golf. Though, you can also supplement water with green juices, smoothies, fruit, and berries. All of these can help you stay hydrated while at the same time being high in vitamins, minerals, and salt(electrons), which you also burn a lot of and can get depleted during your round of golf. However, stay away from juices, softdrinks, candy, and other HIGH sugar or sugar free fluids. They will spike your energy levels and deplete you of your hydration often resulting in a sugar low, which never ends pretty, usually making you become a DRAMA QUEEN.

Hydration levels are individual but as a guideline adults should drink between 1½-2 liters a day - though, more on hot days or when you are playing a round of golf. You should be drinking fluids all day, from morning to evening, and of course on the golf course! Maintaining good levels of hydration before, during and after your round will improve high energy levels for high performances!

# Recovery is the key to top-results!

It is commonly accepted that the way to the top is hard work, the more the better. And this isn't entirely wrong either. However, without proper recovery it is almost impossible to work hard and train effectively day after day. If you put recovery high up on your priority list, your body and your mind will quickly be fit for fight and ready to progress and take you to the next level in your performance. This means that after your round of golf, you need to concentrate on getting your body back in the state it was in before you started the day, which means you need to replenish your hydration levels, your glycogen deposits, and your muscle proteins. In this process nutrition plays a major roll as well as rest. Your body craves energy, and therefore it can be tempting to eat food high in sugar and starch, but this will cause too much of an imbalance in your blood sugar, which increases the risk of inflammation of your muscles and tendons.

# Regulate your blood sugar to WIN!

We are all familiar with the 3pm phenomenon, where you are in dire need of chocolate, sweets, cake, a coke or something with a high sugar content that will help you up again from a serious energy crash! We get stuck in the middle of our busy daily routines and cannot help bumping into the candy jar as our body screams out for quick energy. This is something your brain learned long ago, that the fasted way to get energy comes from sugar, fat, and salts. However, dipping into the candy jar is a guaranteed recipe for disaster as this will result in an even deeper dive of energy, causing lack of concentration and frustration. We all know that this is not the perfect situation if you have just double bogeyed the 9th and you have still got to play the backnine. In this situation it is ALL about regulating your blood sugar. From now on in your blood sugar is the most important factor in how you will perform down the home stretch before reaching the clubhouse. But how do you know if your levels are getting depleted? Well the symptoms are often felt as getting hungry, or tired or lethargic or even being easily irritated and throwing your clubs in the water of the lovely greenside lake on the 9th. When your blood sugar is regulated, you feel alive, full of happiness, alert and energetic. Blood sugar is the name used for the glucose that we all have in our blood. Glucose is a type of sugar, but it is not to be confused with the sugar we can consume. Blood sugar is our body's constant supplier of an moderate level of energy to our muscles and our brain.

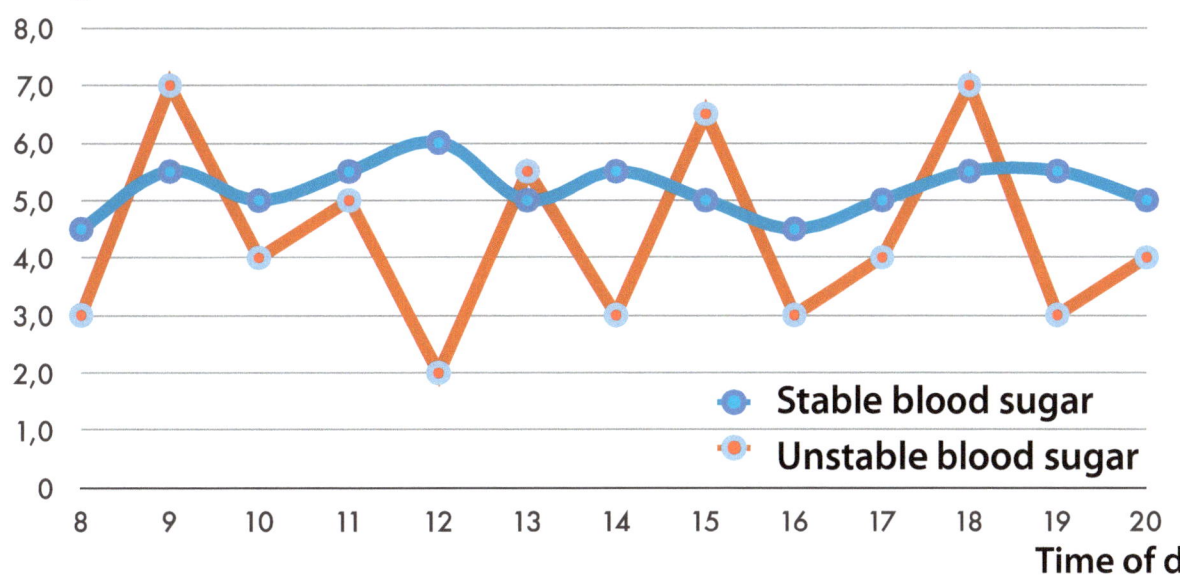

Unfortunately the food being eaten in this generation is a blood sugar nightmare like never seen before. It has become a full blown epidemic that is caused by refined carbohydrates, which is put in, cakes, sugar, softdrinks, alcohol, cereals, fastfoods, microwavable foods, pasta, breads and much more.

Many manufacturers have even started labeling their goods as healthy by giving them misleading titles and putting pictures of fit people on them. Diabetes is often the result of this unhealthy lifestyle, however, there are many people that suffer from having blood sugar problems that do not have diabetes. Our body flourishes with a average blood sugar level of 5,5 mmol. After a good nights sleep we have an average of 3,5 to 4,5 mmol. Then it increases when we eat breakfast. If we eat a good balanced breakfast for example egg, Greek yoghurt, muesli with seeds and nuts, oatmeal with fresh berries and a glass of water, our blood sugar will climb smoothly to 5,5 mmol and stay balanced with a steady and stable release of insulin. If we eat white bread with marmalade, a couple cups of coffee, or perhaps some pancakes our blood sugar increases rapidly and gets too high stressing our body and our pancreas, which in turn releases a large amount of insulin. We experience a quick high, though looming around the corner is a huge low, which we feel as exhaustion and poor concentration.

## Symptoms of having unstable bloodsugar

- Craving sweets and soft drinks
- Feeling better after eating.
- Feeling bad or bonking, when you do not get food on time.
- Experiencing nausea or anorexia- especially in the morning.
- Extreme thirst.
- Hungry after eating a meal.
- Crave salt, fat, or alcohol.
- Feeling faint or exhausted.
- Tremoring/ inner turmoil
- Energy levels and mood swings fluctuate between high and low all day.

## Tips to stay on tops in regulating your blood sugar

- Eat no less than 3 meals a day, or even more often, 5-7 meals of lesser portion.
- Exercise atleast a half an hour a day.
- Eat plenty of food that are high in fiber.
- Stop eating sugar or sugar free products, instead eat honey, berries, or fruit for sweetness.
- Stay away from all raffined grains and cereal products.
- Eat berries, apples, oranges, grapefruits, kiwi and melons instead of dried fruits.
- Eat proteins of high quality such as chicken, fish, turkey, beef, pork, lamb, game, beans, chickpeas, quinoa, lenses, nuts, and almonds.
- Be sure to eat a good portion of healthy fats each day, especially omega 3 fats such as fish, avocado, nuts, almonds, and linseed.

# The nutritional plate of champions

YES, nutrition is extremely important to your well being on and off the golf course! But how do you know if you are eating a balanced diet? Try using this nutritional plate as a guidline. By eating these suggestions on a daily basis you will be providing your body with the nutrients, minerals, and vitamins that are necessary to live a balanced diet that will lead to performance at the highest level. On top of choosing the correct foods from this plate, be reasonable and respect your bodys signals of hunger, thurst, and knowing when you are filled so you do not over eat.

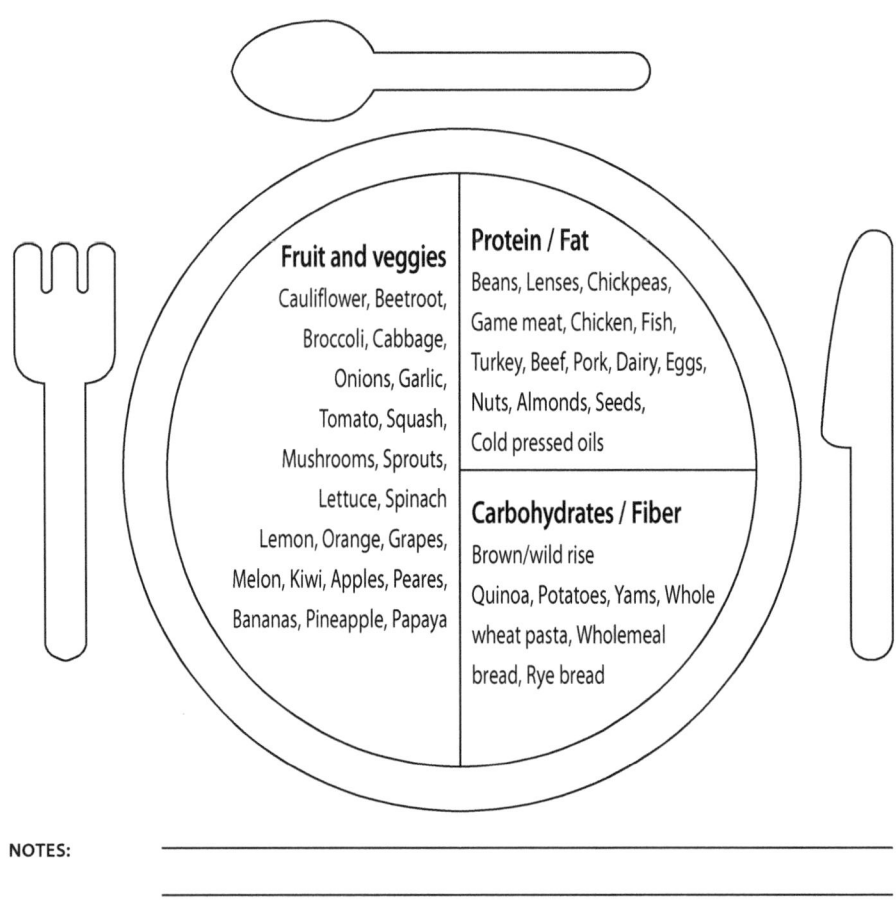

**Fruit and veggies**
Cauliflower, Beetroot, Broccoli, Cabbage, Onions, Garlic, Tomato, Squash, Mushrooms, Sprouts, Lettuce, Spinach Lemon, Orange, Grapes, Melon, Kiwi, Apples, Peares, Bananas, Pineapple, Papaya

**Protein / Fat**
Beans, Lenses, Chickpeas, Game meat, Chicken, Fish, Turkey, Beef, Pork, Dairy, Eggs, Nuts, Almonds, Seeds, Cold pressed oils

**Carbohydrates / Fiber**
Brown/wild rise
Quinoa, Potatoes, Yams, Whole wheat pasta, Wholemeal bread, Rye bread

NOTES: _____

PERNILLE H. STEENBERG ©

89

## Healthy Fats are GOOD!

Omega-3 fatty acids are healthy supplements that you need to add in your diet, because the can reduce inflammation in your tendons and muscles, which is a common problem for golfers. Both because of the endurance of the long walks during your round but also the huge amount of stress your body endures under the explosive movement of the golf swing. You will find Omega-3 fatty acids in foods such as fish high in fat, leafy vegetables, eggs and walnuts. It is also a good idea to add supplements to your diet such as fish oils like cod liver oils.

# 6 Simple Diet changes that will make you healthier!

Living healthier does not always mean that you need to make a huge alteration to your diet! In fact it is often the little things that make the big differences in living a healthier lifestyle.

**Here are 6 popular foods that your can easily replaced with a healthier alternatives**

1. White bread baked with sifted wheat flour: can be replaced with Dark breads that have added seeds and or nuts.

2. Candy and sweets that have added sugar, artificial sweeteners, dyes, additives: can be replaced with fruits, berries, dried fruit, smoothies, nuts, almonds, and chocolate with minimum of 70% cacao.

3. Soft drinks both with sugar and artificial sweeteners: can be replaced with sparkling water with lemon, fruit juices without added sugar, chilled green tea, homemade juicers and shakes, or tapwater with for example a cinnamon stick, lemon grass, cucumber, or anise added.

4. Canned Mackerel and tuna in cheap oils: Can be replaced with fresh fish, tuna in water/olive oil, stock fish, frozen shrimp or old fashioned matured herring.

5. Pre-prepared cake mixes, sauces and soups: can be replaced with homemade cakes, sauces made from scratch with good ingredients, and homemade soups that can be frozen down.

6. Refined oils, oils in plastic bottles, mayonnaise or something similar that is made of refined vegetable oils and fats: can be replaced with cold pressed virgin oils made of for example olives, sunflower seeds, thistle, sesame, linseed, or rapeseed oil. Also organic mayonnaise made of virgin oils, preferable homemade.

# Colorful fruits, berries, and vegetables

Fruits, berries and vegetables all contribute with high levels of nutrients in your diet. Infact many years of research and studies prove that people that eat alot of fruit and vegetables as opposed to those who do not, will reduce in their chances of having cancer by half, as well as drastically reducing the risk of cardio vascular diseases. Fruits, berries, and vegetables contain plenty of fiber, carbohydrates, vitamins, minerals and antioxidants that strengthen your immune system. Most fruits, berries and vegetables contain fluids that help the body maintain hydrated. The sweetness in them can also help stop that craving for junk food.

Fruits, berries and vegetables can be eaten alone or as a snack between meals, as a main course, or as a dessert. Yes the possibilities are endless. When possible it is a great idea to combine nuts, seeds or avocado to add proteins and fats to your colorful fruits and veggies - Mmmm, good!

# Breakfast of CHAMPIONS!

Everybody knows that breakfast is the most important meal of the day, but here is a special recipe for homemade muesli that will guarantee you start your day with an extra swagger in your walk!

- 1 dl. Oatmeal
- 1 dl. Spelt flakes
- 1 dl. Chopped almonds and hazelnuts
- 1 dl. Sunflower seeds and dried pumpkinseeds

Now mix the ingredients and lay them flat out on baking paper and put it in the oven at a low temperature until they are lightly browned. Add a tablespoon of quality honey if you want extra flavor.

Add
- 1 tbsp. coconut flour
- 1 tbsp. pure cinnamon (without sugar)
- Possible. ½ tsp. Vanilla powder (not vanilla sugar)
- Possible. 1 tbsp. Sesame seeds.

If you want to sweeten your muesli, then add freshly sliced fruit, fresh berries or dried fruit like apricots, figs or raisins. Serve on top of natural yogurt like Greek yogurt. Be sure to make enough for the whole week, it can be stored in a seal tight jar, so that it is ready to serve when you are ready for it! Now that is fast and easy, there can be no excuses that you did not have time to eat breakfast!

# Lunch that is simple, healthy and tastes great!

In order for your mind and body to run efficiently, both on and off the golf course, you will need premium fuel. The bonus of making your own lunch is that you will know exactly what kind of fuel you will be running on, and you will lessen the chances of opting for the quick fix of fastfood or other unhealthy choices. Sugar and refined carbohydrates in the form of white bread, pasta, and some yoghurts with added flavors leave you with an unstable blood sugar, which as we know drastically affects our energy levels and concentration throughout the day. On the opposite side of the menu, we know that essential fatty acids, fiber, good proteins, and water help make us feel energetic and will increase our levels of concentration. The easiest way to make a healthy lunch is simply to use the leftovers from last night's dinner. When you are making dinner, simple cut a few extra veggies and salad so that you have an extra portion for your lunch. It could be carrots, peppers, cucumber, cherry tomatoes, fresh spinach leaves, cauliflower or other tasty stuff that can be put on a dark bread sandwich. Just fill your lunch up with a ton of energy-giving vegetables, then you can always add some grass-fed meats and of course be sure to spread a healthy layer of grass-fed butter on that dark brown bread, mmmm good! It really is not that difficult, and as long as the quality of the foods you are using is good, then the food will always have alot of flavor and the benefits will be rewarding.

Another great idea for your lunch is slow rising breads as seen on the next page. This is a great bread to eat everyday and is guaranteed to give you pleasure. You will feel that you are eating raw energy when you sink your teeth into it and your body will thank you for it! This portion will make 15-20 rolls or 2-3 flutes.

**Slow rising bread with sesame, sunflower seeds, and linseed.**
- 1 l of water
- 10 g. yeast (about the size of 2 peas)
- 1 tbsp. salt
- 200 g. wholemeal flour
- 200 g. oatmeal
- Approx. 200 g. sesame seeds, sunflower seeds and linseed
- 2 grated carrots
- approx. 200 grams high quality wheat flour
- 4.5 tbsp. of cold-pressed olive oil

Start by dissolving the yeast in the water. Now add the rest of the ingredients (except for the olive oil) and knead it together to make dough. Pour the olive oil on top and cover with a dishtowel and leave it overnight to rise (8-10 hours). Then shape the dough into rolls or flutes with a spoon and place them on baking paper on a tray. Bake it at 200degrees Celcius for about 30 minutes. Check frequently the first time, as there is often differences in ovens. You can also choose to half bake it then put in the freezer so that it can be heated and baked finished at a later date.

# Tasty snacks to ease YOUR hunger!

When you want to perform at your best on the golf course throughout your entire round, it is a good idea to supplement your lunch with some snacks in between holes. Here is a healthy suggestion:
Almonds and raisins in cocao and cinnimon.
This is a great alternative to replacing that chocolate bar that will spike your blood sugar levels out of control.
- 3 dl. almonds
- 3 dl. dark raisins
- 3-4 tbls. of raw cacao powder
- 2 tbls. of ground cinnamon

Mix the almonds, raisins, cacao, and cinnamon thoroughly in a plastic bag or tin.

# Post round and training

Within a half hour after completing your round of golf or training you need to eat foods high in carbohydrates. A homemade smoothie that is high in carbohydrates and will help replenish your hydration levels is the perfect choice. Also eat some almonds that are high in proteins and fats.
Here is a recipe for a good homemade smoothie that you can make at home before your round and then store in the clubhouse's canteen.

In this recipe you will need a 1 L. blender.

- 300 g. frozen blueberries & rasberries
- 2 oranges
- 2-4 dates (to give it sweetness)
- 1 banana
- 1 sprinkle of vanilla powder
- cold water (add the right amount to create the perfect texture for you).

Mix all the ingredients in the blender, then add 1 scoop of rice protein power and 2 table spoons of Omega 3 oil.

## The EXPERIMENT: 9 tips in how you will gain more energy from your diet!

Energy surrounds us. We use energy all day, everyday, and it fluctuates throughout the day, the week, the year. Most of us wish for more energy, and luckily our energy is something we are able to control and influence ourselves. Your daily nutritional intake has a huge influence on your energy levels. Would you like to test just how big an impact it makes, then I suggest you experiment and test yourself by trying one or more of the suggestions below!

**#1.** Try to eat a healthy diet 6 out of 7 days, without junk food, sugar, or alcohol. You have to eat natural/organic products without harmful additives that take a heavy toll on your resources to break down all the toxins they create in your system.

**#2.** Eat healthy fatty acids everyday, for example morning shots of orange juice with 1.2tbsp of linseed oils mixed in, or supplement in fish oils or cod liver oils. On top of that plenty of nuts, almonds, avocados, seeds, and delicious cold pressed oils in salads.

**#3.** Eat tons of green vegetables like cabbage, spinach, celleri, parsley, broccoli, rucola, herbs and so on. Green vegetables contain the most energy.

**#4.** Do not over eat your meals, eat until you feel approx. 80% full.

**#5.** Approx. 30% of your daily diet should be raw. Vegetables, fruits, sprouts, and oils. (not meat and other animal products).

**#6.** Give your digestion a break, at least a couple of hours a day. Let your lymphatic system do its job cleaning and rinsing in peace and quiet. Do not eat constantly even if it is healthy snacks.

**#7.** Drink lots of fluids. Drink a big glass of tap water in the morning and then another glass every hour throughout the day. Remember, dehydrating yourself by just 2% of your norm is equal to a loss of 10% of your energy!

**#8.** Stop dieting and starving yourself! It will just set your body into survival mod conserving your energy, which means you will feel as though you have none, and it will not help you lose weight in the long run!

**#9.** When shopping for groceries, ask yourself if this food you are putting in your cart has ever been alive? Is it grown in the ground, on plants, or lived a good life? Food that has lived well has tons of energy!

# Chapter 8:
# The Mental game
## (getting out of your own way)

Staying mentally on top of your game can be one of the toughest obstacles to overcome while working on improving your game. We often remind ourselves on the course that this game is not easy and become failure-conscious rather than success-conscious at the worst possible moments.

Remember, as a golfer you are without a doubt an athlete, and the greatest athletes in the world are the greatest not because of their natural abilities, but because of their mental ability to overcome obstacles. Here is a little story about one of the world's best basketball players, Michael Jordan. Now the story goes that he was cut from his high school basketball team, understandably he was disappointed. Michaels gift was not entirely his natural born talent, but the gift of acceptance and devotion to overcome defeat. This man had a dream that was perhaps fueled by failure. When someone tells you that you can not do something and that you are not good enough, how many of you say, oh that is a shame or bummer, and accept that it was not meant to be? Or even worse, you tell yourself that you can not suceed because you do not like the feeling of failure, so it is easier to tell yourself to quit before you embarrass yourself. Failure is tough to overcome, but at some point everybody will face failure in doing something. When failure strikes you have only two choices;

Choice one

Make excuses for your failure, feeling bad inside and not able to let go of the negative feelings and eventually give up on your dreams, afterall you probably were not good enough anyways.

Choice two

You pick yourself up again because you are worth it, that dream is worth it, you want it so bad that you are focused on the process involved in achieving it and not the individual victories or defeats. Because failure is nothing more than another speed bump on your road to success. Every successful athlete has learned to overcome failure; it is a skill that you can and need to learn if you want to become successful. Michael was fueled by his defeat. It just made him want his dream even more. Now the easiest way to tackle defeat is to forget about it and focus on the process ahead. That is right! You will need to check your mental baggage at the door! Later on in his carrier when Michael's team lost a game, the coach would talk to the team in the locker room (as they do). Telling the players what they did wrong, but Michael was able to evaluate and check his mental baggage within 15 minutes after the game, so that he could overcome those negative feelings of defeat because he knew that the only way to stay mentally strong was to fill himself up with more fuel and stay focused and look forward to another week of quality training in preparation for next week's game.

Many believe that Jack Nicklaus is the best golfer that this world has produced so far. Jack was a guest of honor at a presentation to which he was asked in public about a tournament that he had lost by one stroke a week earlier "Jack, do you believe you lost the tournament because of the three putt you made on the 18th hole on the final day." Jack's response was, "I'm sorry sir, but you are mistaking, I have never three putted the final hole on the final day of a tournament."

Our world is full of people who are great at reminding us of our mistakes, instead of reminding us of our successes! Negative people and their thoughts and insecurities can infect you like a virus. So surround yourself with positive people that have positive thoughts and are willing to remind you of your good shots and experiences and before you know it, you will be ignoring the negative comments and remembering the positive thoughts on your own.

# Believing in yourself!

### Accepting the unacceptable

As I mentioned earlier in the book, expectations can lead to frustration, frustration can lead to anger, temper tantrums, and usually lose of confidence. You have to learn to accept bad shots so that you can stay focused on the task at hand and at the same time enjoy yourself. Keeping a calm acceptance of things and a positive attitude when playing poorly will not guarantee your game will improve, but it will guarantee that you will play better than if you stay negative, angry, and frustrated with yourself. Do not ever forget, something about this game must have enticed you and given you pleasure, so be careful not to take golf so seriously that you forget to enjoy yourself out there!

### Loving the challenge!

When the best players in the world are playing their best, they are inlove with golf, understanding that golf is not a game of perfect. They can play a sort of game that is called "Hit it, find it, then hit it again!" Never losing focus and always loving the challenge of the next shot, a sort of poetry of the golfing gods!

### Avoid golfers Insanity!

When people are not in touch with reality, they can become a danger to themselves and others, so we call them clinically insane and lock them up! When you lose touch with reality, your mind wanders, and you are no longer living in the "now". By not staying in the moment, you begin to worry and you become a danger to yourself and your golf game! Worrying is a socially accepted sign that you are on the verge of insanity! If you keep thinking of what has already happened or worrying about what might happen in the future, you are not living in reality. Golf cannot be played to its best if you keep thinking about that double bogey you just had on the previous hole or fear of what might happen on the next shot or hole, you have to live in the now! Take it one shot at a time, and stay rooted in reality, in the now! By worrying about what has not happened and may never happen, you are actually behaving insanely, yes that is right, you may be insane!

Are you worried about flying, about the plane crashing, then think about this; do you enjoy worrying? Do you feel good about yourself when you worry or feel sick to your stomach? So let us say that you have booked a flight, and a week before leaving you are nervous, all week, worrying, worrying, worrying. Then you take your flight and arrive safely at your destination - you made it! What if you decided not to worry the week before your next flight? Would your life not be better? You would definately feel better. You might even enjoy yourself and look forward to your journey! Next time think positive and if the plane does crash, would your worries have made a difference? Get out of bed - live life and stop worrying!

*So for Pete's sake*
- ***Accept the unacceptable,***
- ***Love every challenge,***
- ***and stay sane!***

# Chapter 9:
# Arrival on time! (Checking out)

No shortcuts to success here but by doing and following this book correctly, you are ensuring that your golf game and swing are on the path to being healthier and more efficient. By earning the right to a more efficient body you are in fact taking a shortcut to improvement. The alternative being that you choose not to improve your body's quality of movement, which will lead to a less efficient way to improvement and way of life. So now that you understand more about yourself and how YOU can easily improve your golf game, if you decide not to improve your bodys quality of movement and healthy diet then you are actually self willingly deciding to take the long route to improvement. That is if you improve at all!! Does anyone actually enjoy willingly doing things less efficiently? That would be like having a wheel barrel full of rocks that you needed to move, but instead of transporting the rocks in the wheel barrel, you decide to tip the rocks out of the wheel barrel and carry them one by one! Be smart people, take the wheel barrel, take the shortcut and improve your body to improve your golf swing and your life!

I sincerely hope you have enjoyed learning how you can be your best, in golf, and in life! If there are any questions that you have, please drop me an email and I will do my best to get back to you.
adamstevensongolf@mail.com

# A Special thank you!

I would like to thank the great team I have around me for helping me. Especially my beautiful wife, and my friends and family for supporting me, and pretty much encouraging me to be the ME I am today.

Special thanks to the guys at TPI and to Jason Glass for teaching me to Dream Big and Overdeliver! Your teachings has helped me to understand the things I do, and kept me inspired and interested in exploring new things on a continual path of learning and teaching.

*"In golf as in life it is the follow through that makes the difference"*
- *Unidentified author*